Spanish Guitar Classics

35 Pieces in standard notation and tablature

Compiled and edited by
Dmitrijs Volkovs

Miller 2025

Copyright © 2025 Dmitrijs Volkovs

ISBN: 978-1-7641097-7-2

CONTENTS

1 Leyenda Theme *(Isaac Albeniz)*
3 Romance *(Anonymous)*
5 Allegretto *(Dionisio Aguado)*
7 Waltz *(Dionisio Aguado)*
9 Siciliano *(Dionisio Aguado)*
11 Allegro *(Dionisio Aguado)*
13 Waltz *(Fernando Sor)*
14 Andante *(Fernando Sor)*
16 Etude No.9 op.35 *(Fernando Sor)*
18 Etude n°14 op.35 *(Fernando Sor)*
20 Etude n°17 op.35 *(Fernando Sor)*
22 Etude No.22 Op.35 *(Fernando Sor)*
24 Andante *(Fernando Sor)*
26 Bolero *(Julian Arcas)*
29 Tango No.1 *(Julian Arcas)*
31 Tango No.4 *(Julian Arcas)*
32 Ejercicio *(Jose Ferrer)*
34 EL Amable *(Jose Ferrer)*
36 Tango n°3 op.50 *(Jose Ferrer)*
38 Pasa-Calle *(José Viñas)*
40 Polka *(José Viñas)*
42 Lagrima *(Francisco Tarrega)*
44 Adelita *(Francisco Tarrega)*
45 Estudio *(Francisco Tarrega)*
47 Etude *(Francisco Tarrega)*
49 Etude No.1 *(Francisco Tarrega)*
51 Marieta *(Francisco Tarrega)*
55 Mazurka En sol *(Francisco Tarrega)*
58 Capricho Arabe *(Francisco Tarrega)*
62 El Testament d'Amélia *(arr. Miguel Llobet)*
64 El Noi de la Mare *(arr. Miguel Llobet)*
66 Leyenda *(Isaac Albéniz)*
75 La Maja de Goya *(Enrique Granados)*
79 Andaluza – *Spanish Dance No.5* *(Enrique Granados)*
81 Serenata Española *(Joaquín Malats)*

Isaac Albéniz (1860 – 1909)

Isaac Albéniz was a Spanish virtuoso pianist, composer, and conductor.
Transcriptions of many of his pieces, such as Asturias(Leyenda), Granada, Sevilla, Cadiz, Córdoba, Cataluña, Mallorca, and Tango in D, are important pieces for classical guitar, though he never composed for the guitar. Some of Albéniz's personal papers are held in the Library of Catalonia.

Below is a simplified version of this play; you can find the advanced version at the end of this book.

Leyenda Theme

Isaac Albeniz (1860-1909)

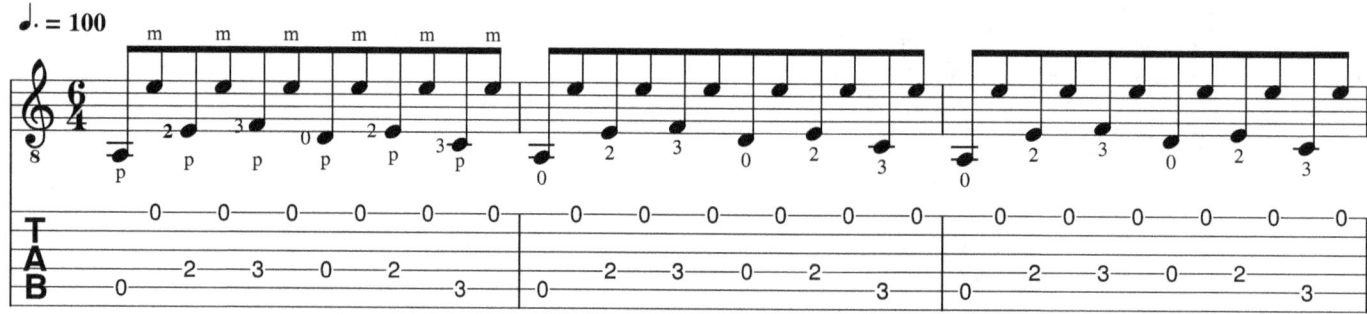

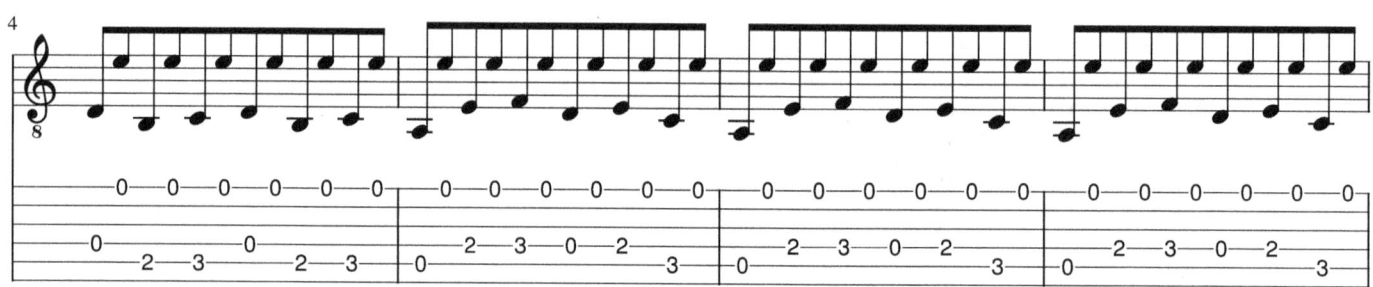

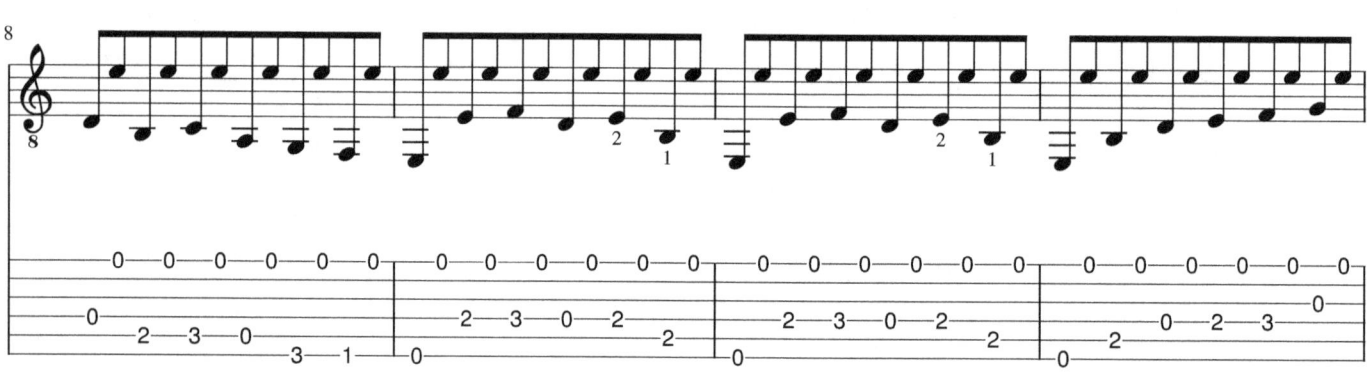

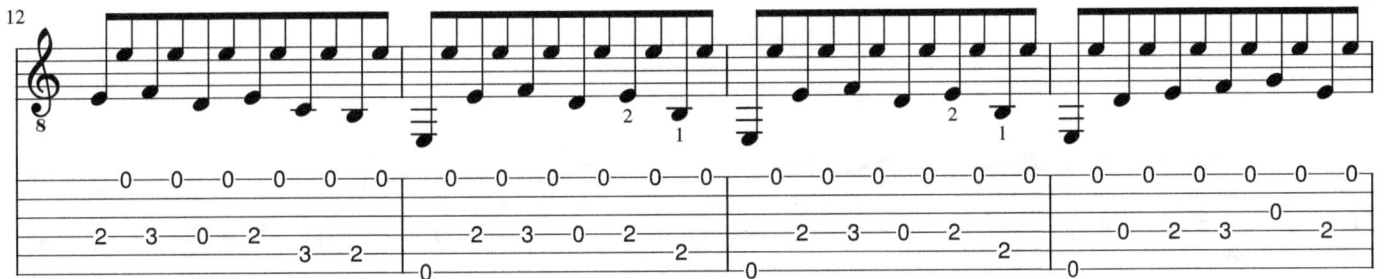

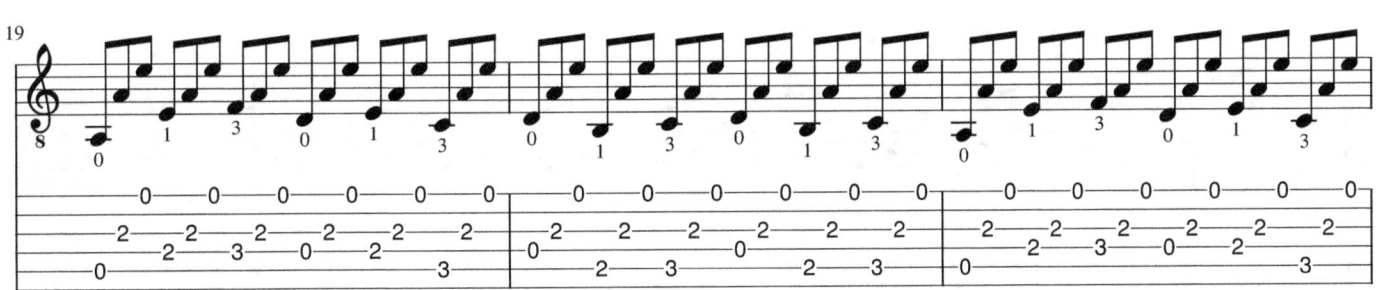
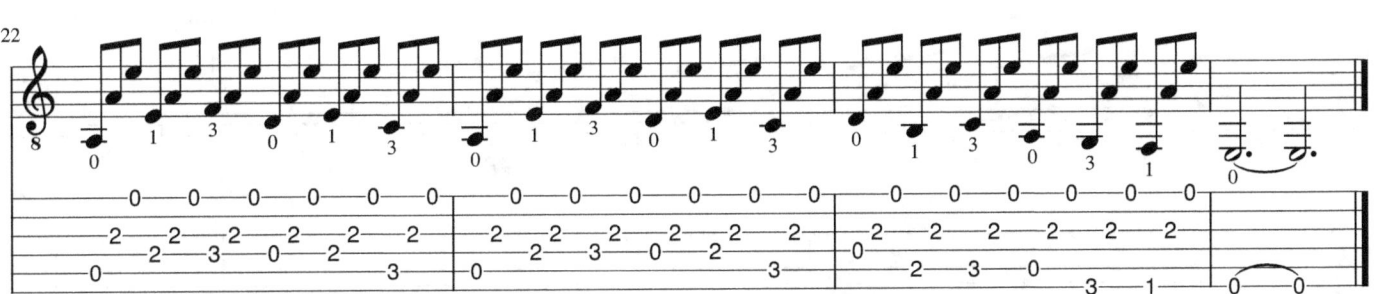

Romance
Spanish Romance

Anonymous

Dionisio Aguado (1784-1849)

Dionisio Aguado was a Spanish classical guitarist and composer. Born in Madrid, he studied with Miguel Garcia. In 1825, Aguado visited Paris, where he met and became friends with lived with Fernando Sor. Aguado's major work Escuela de Guitarra was a guitar tutorial published in 1825. Dionisio Aguado has attained lasting fame through his method for guitar, which is still in print today.

Allegretto

Dionisio Aguado (1784-1849)

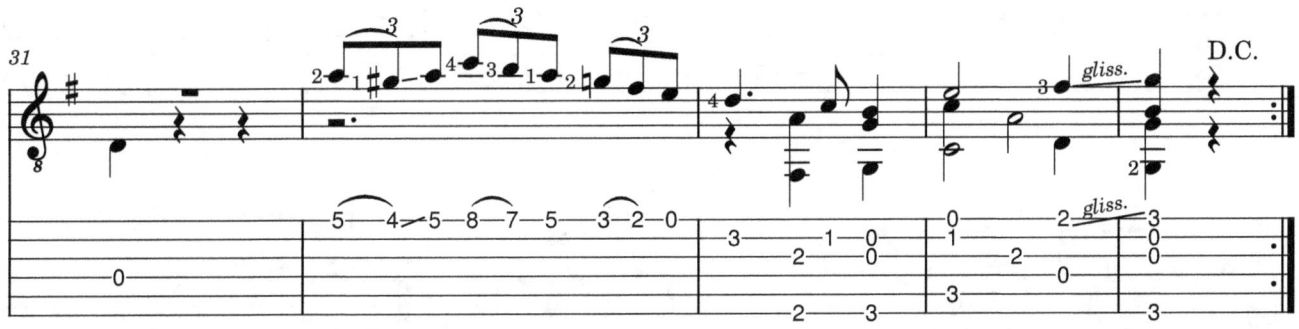

Waltz

Dionisio Aguado (1784-1849)

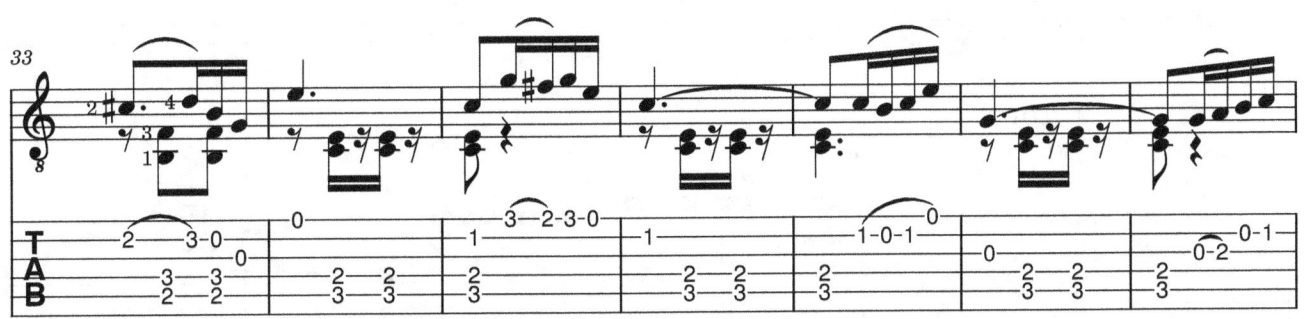

Siciliano

Dionisio Aguado (1784-1849)

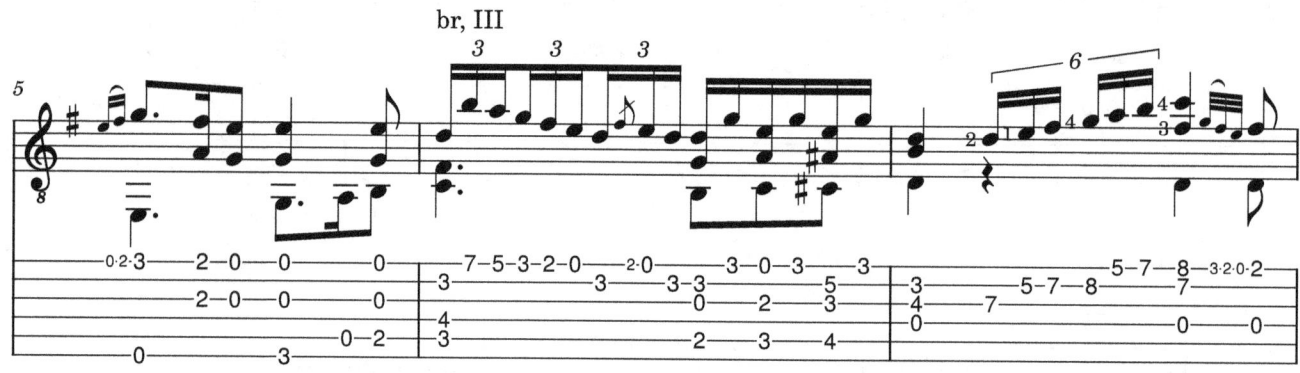

ALLEGRO

Dionisio Aguado (1784-1849)

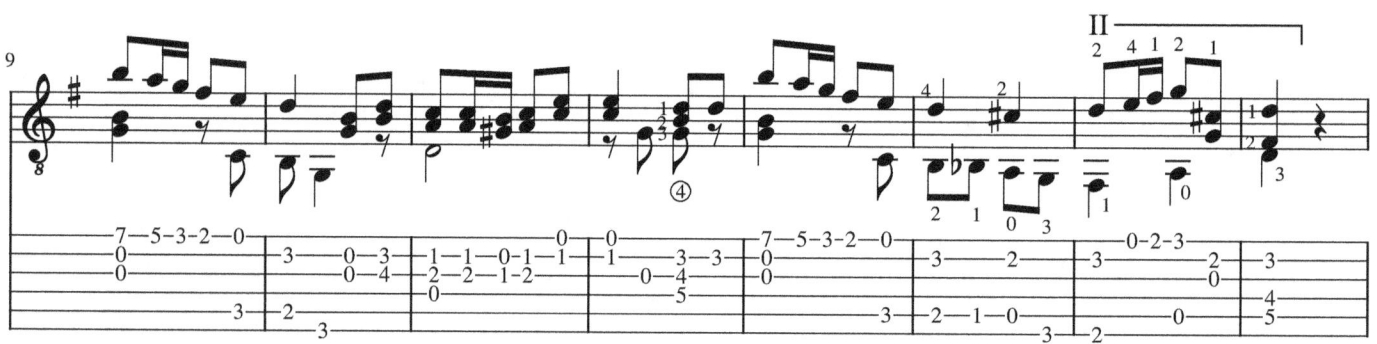

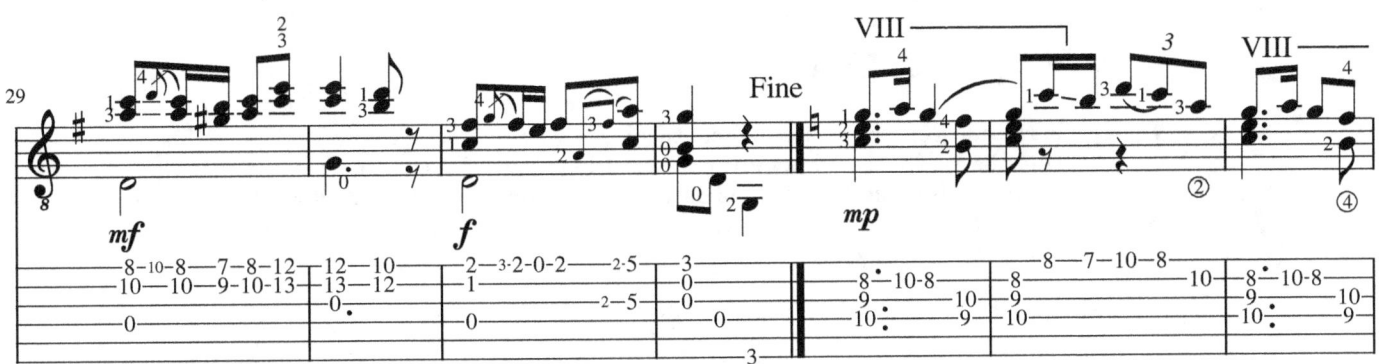

Fernando Sor (1778-1839)

Fernando Sor was a Spanish classical guitarist and composer.
He is best known for his guitar compositions, but he also composed music for opera and ballet, earning acclaim for his ballet titled Cendrillon. Sor's works for guitar range from pieces for advanced players, such as Variations on a Theme of Mozart, to beginner pieces.

Waltz

Fernando Sor (1778-1839)

ANDANTE

Fernando Sor (1778 – 1839)

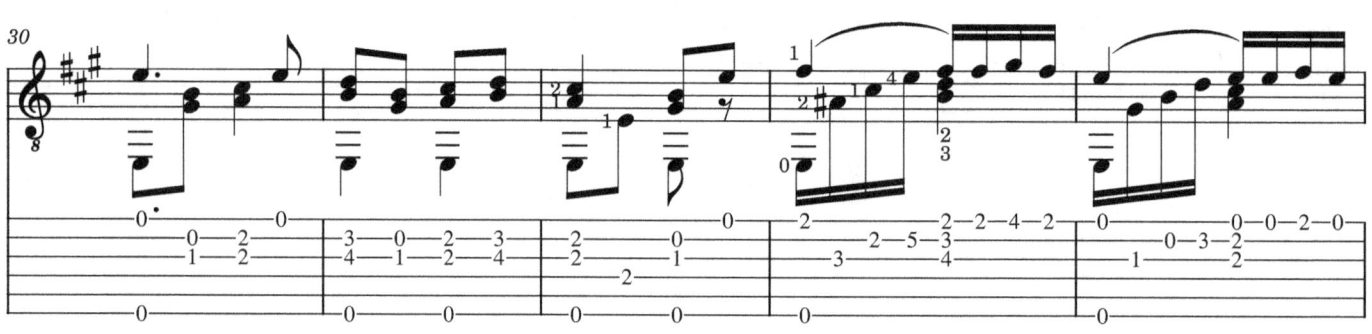
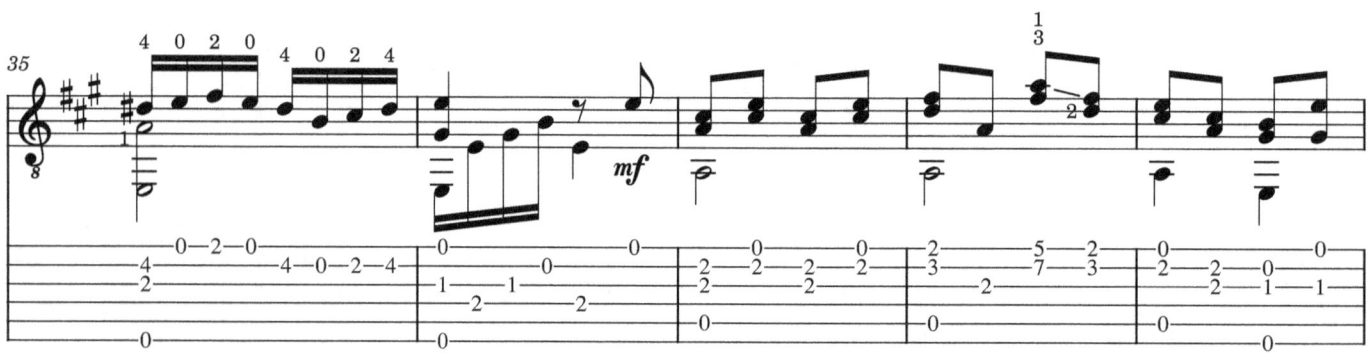
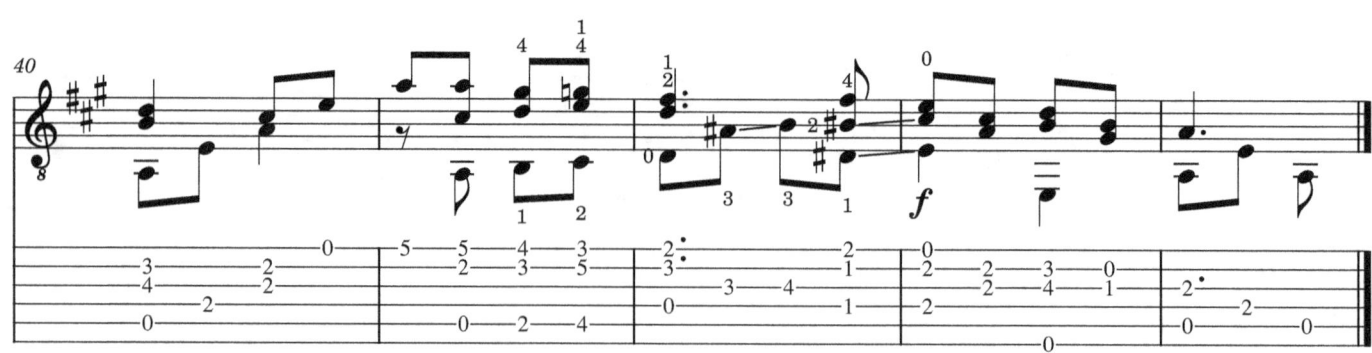

Etude No.9 op.35

Fernando Sor (1778-1839)

Andante.

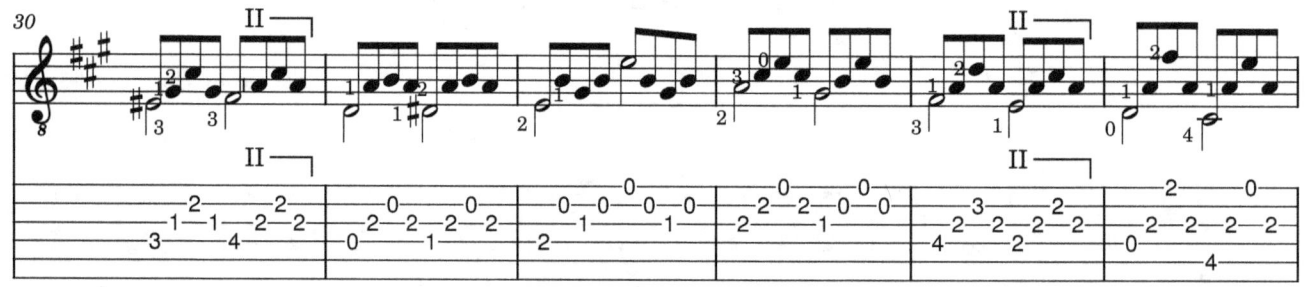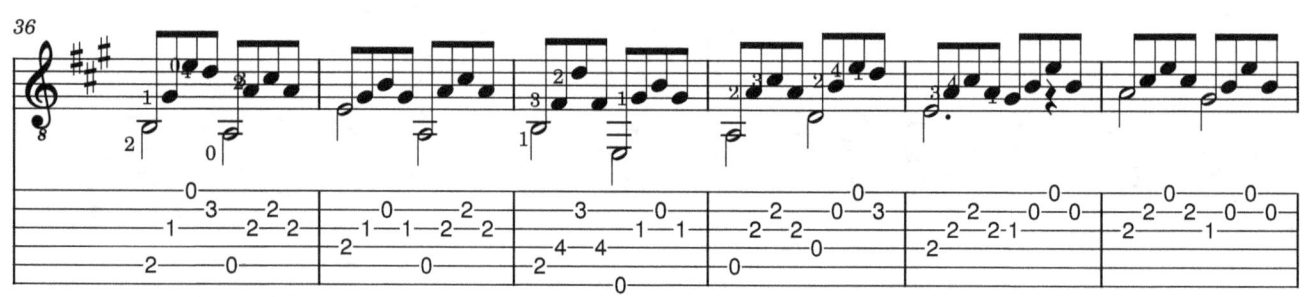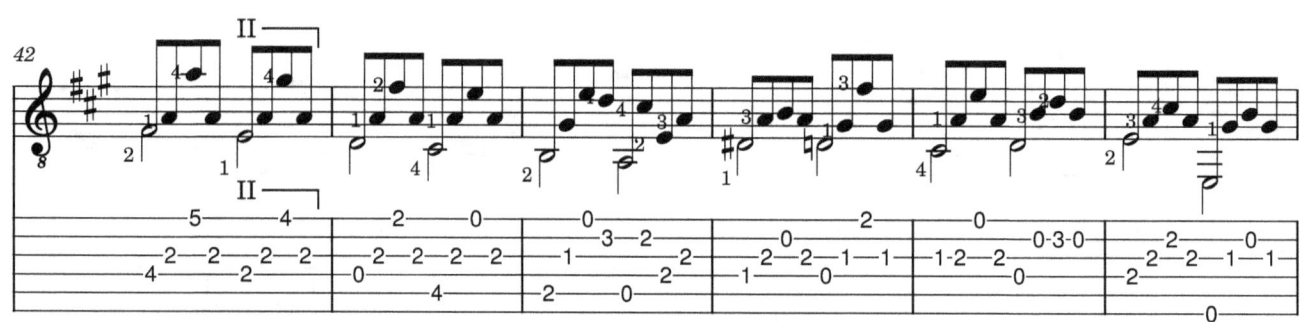

Etude n°14 op.35

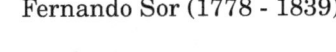

Etude n°17 op.35

Fernando Sor (1778 - 1839)

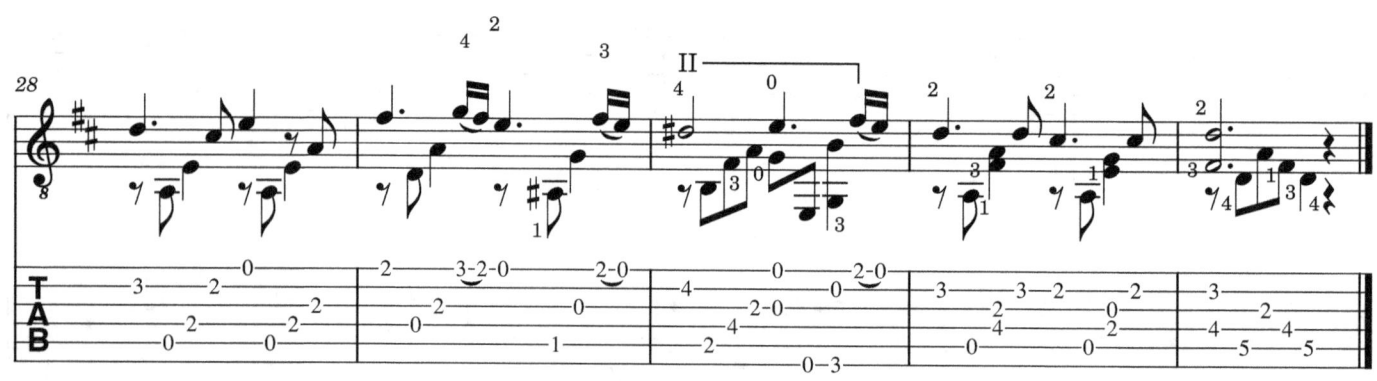

21

Etude No.22 Op.35

Fernando Sor (1778 - 1839)

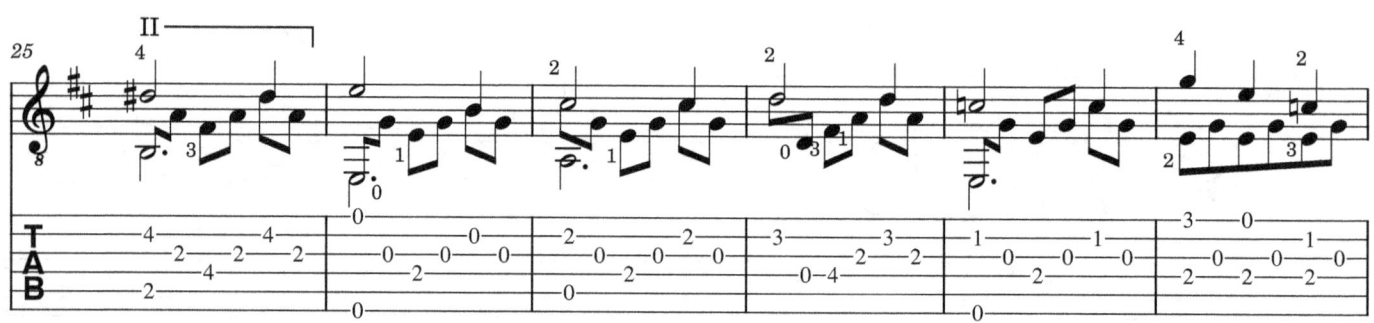

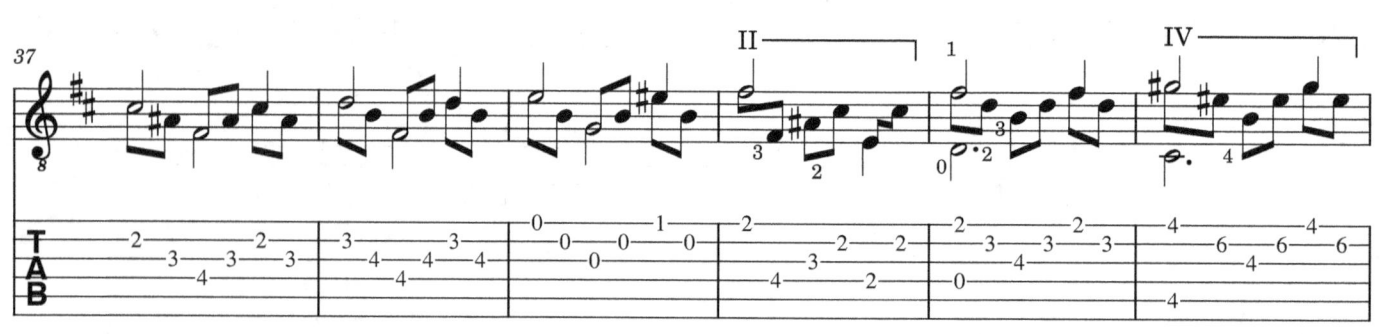

23

Andante

Fernando Sor (1778 - 1839)

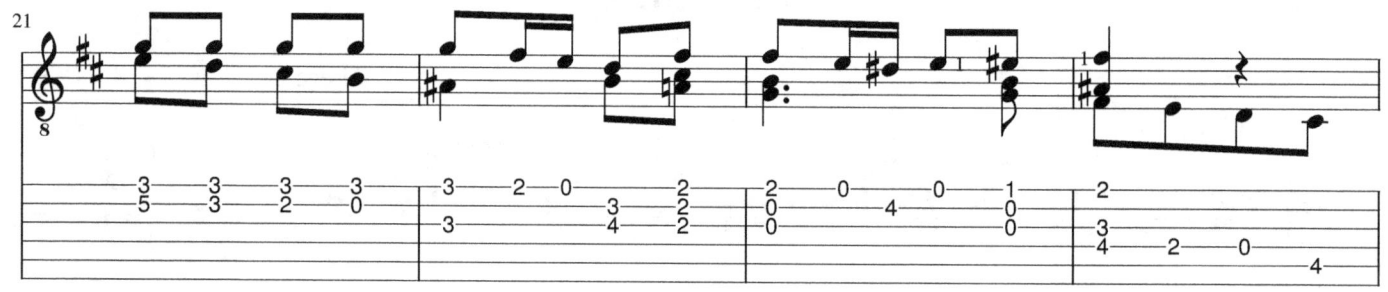

25

Julián Arcas (1832-1882)

Julián Arcas was a Spanish classical guitarist and composer, who influenced Francisco Tárrega and Antonio de Torres. He was "one of the most important figures in Spanish music in the 19th century".

Bolero

Julian Arcas (1832 - 1882)

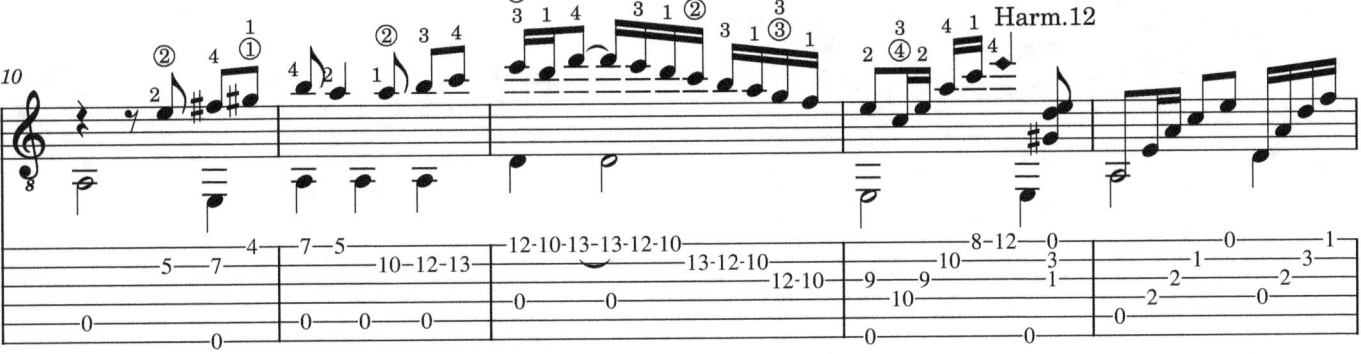

Tango No.1

Aire de Tango

Julian Arcas (1832 - 1882)

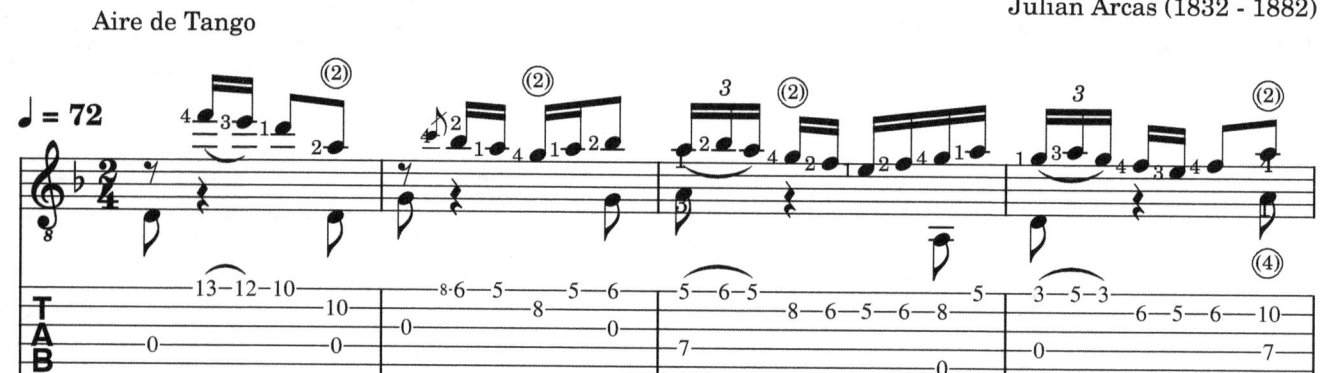
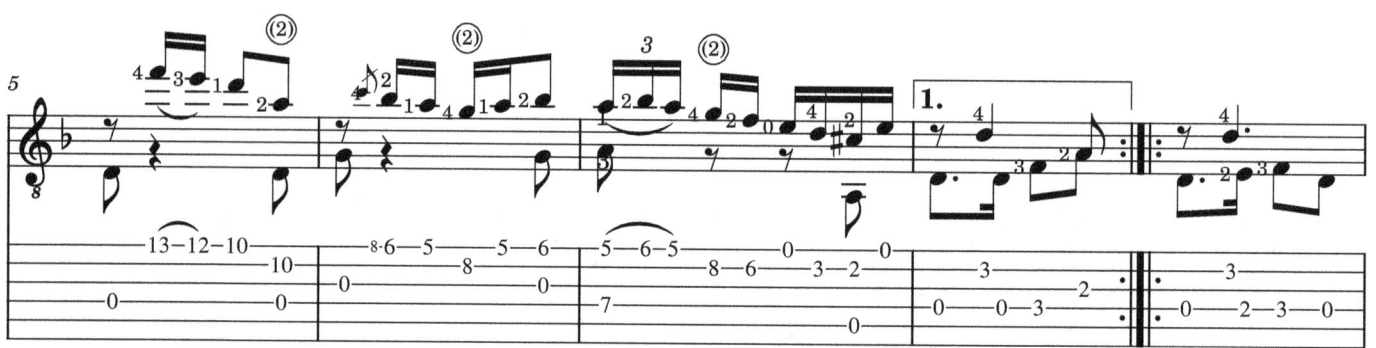

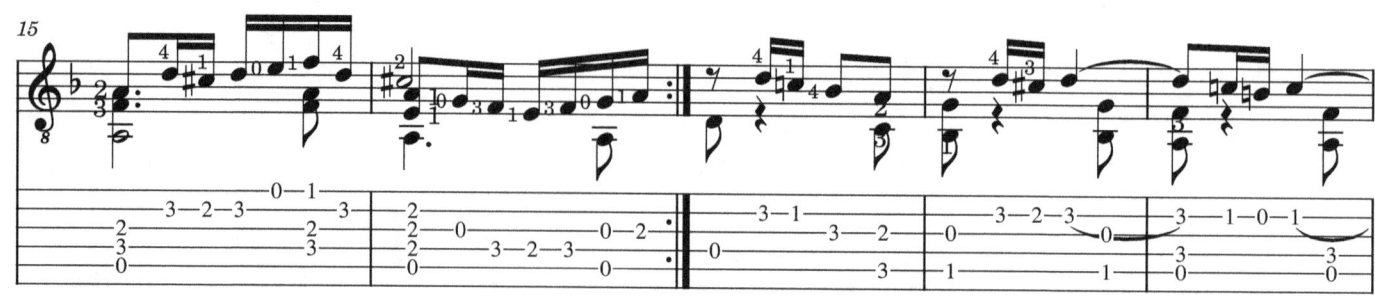

Tango No.4
Coleccion de 5 tangos

Julián Arcas (1832 - 1882)

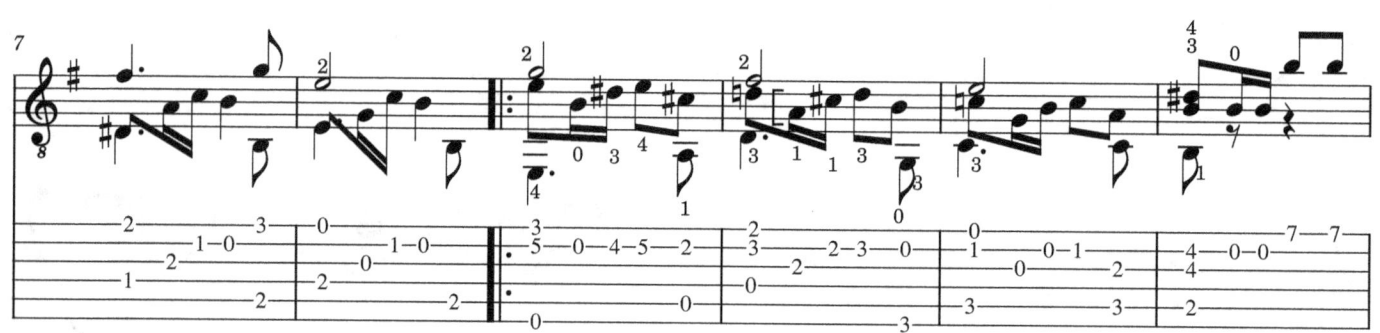

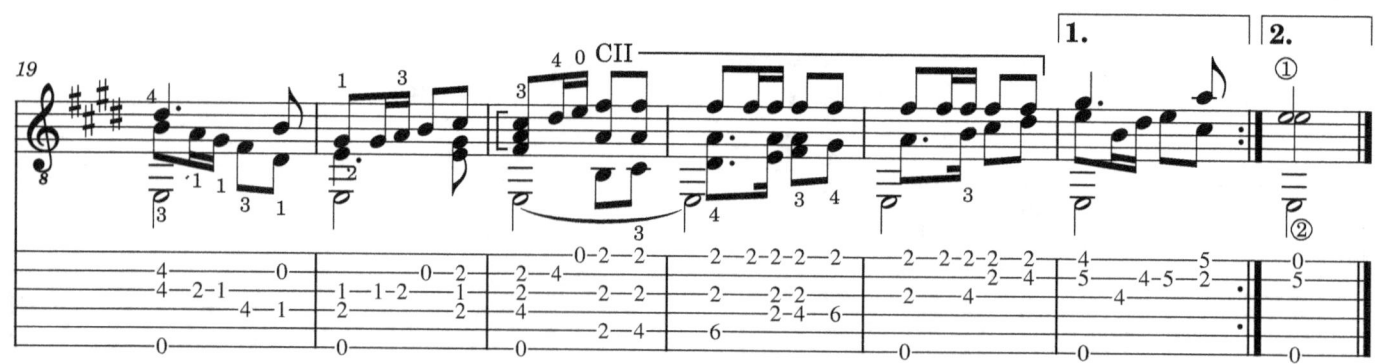

José Ferrer (1835-1916)

José Ferrer was a Spanish guitarist and composer, born in Spain. Ferrer studied guitar with his father, a guitarist and collector of sheet music, before continuing his studies with José Brocá. In 1882, he left Spain for Paris in order to teach at the Institut Rudy and at the Académie Internationale de Musique.

Ejercicio

Jose Ferrer (1835 - 1916)

EL Amable

José Ferrer (1835 - 1916)

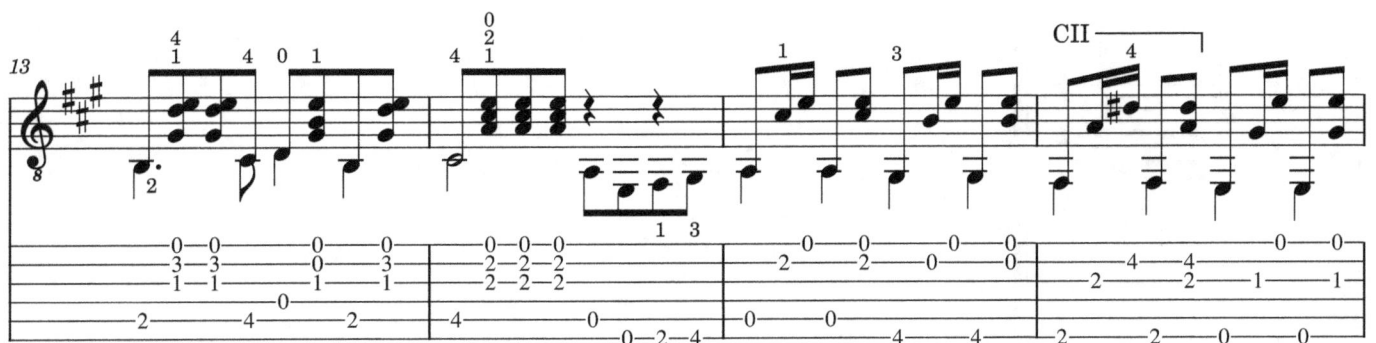

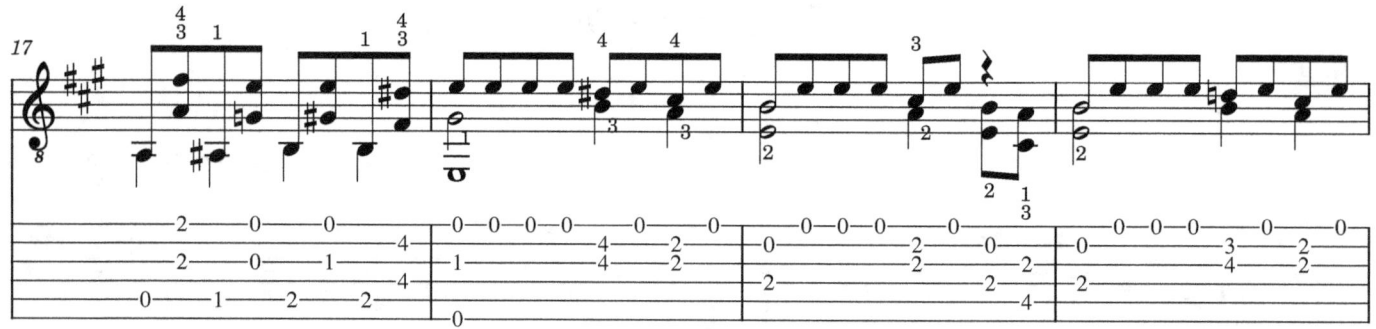

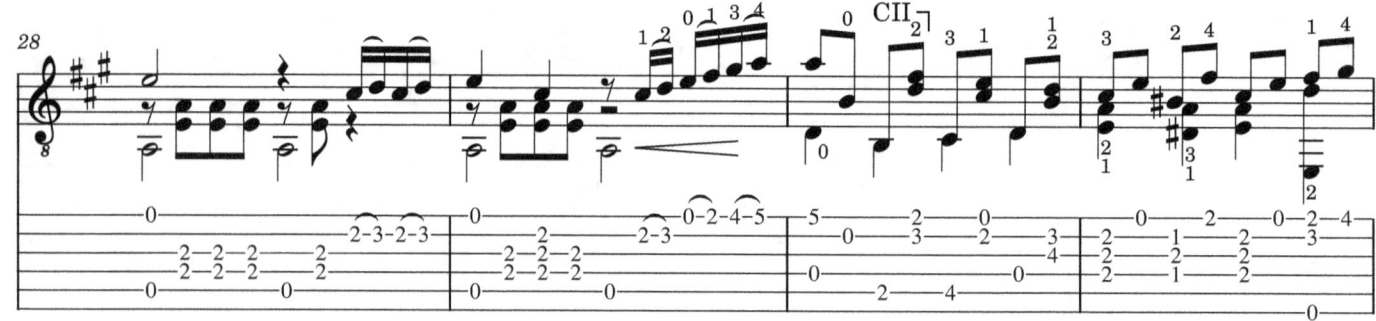
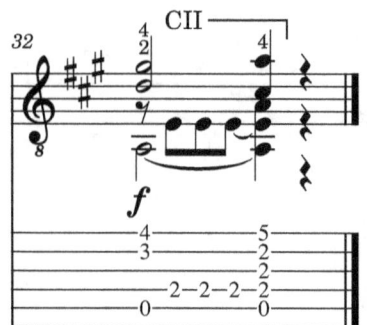

35

Tango n°3 op.50

Jose Ferrer (1835 - 1916)

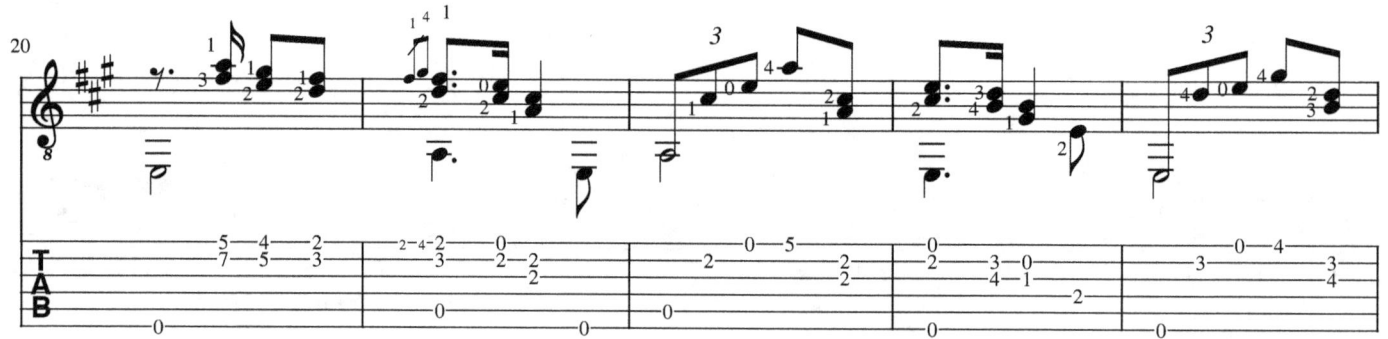

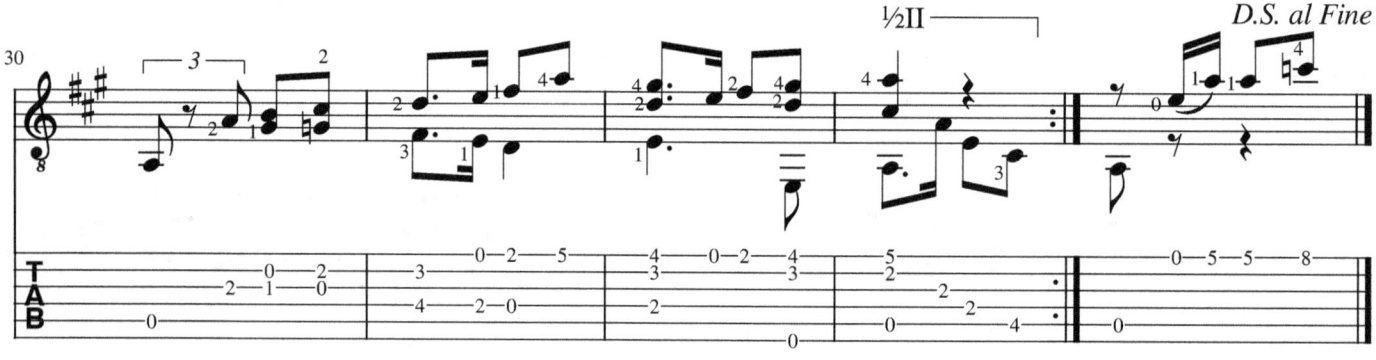

37

Jose Vinas Y Diaz (1823-1888)

Like many of the Spanish top-guitarists of the mid-19th century, his name was overshadowed by Farncisco Tarrega. Nevertheless, Vinas belongs to the group of compser-guitarsts as Jose Broca, Jose Ferrer, Julian Arcas, Juan Parga, Antonio Cano and Jose Costa.

Pasa-Calle

José Viñas (1823-1888)

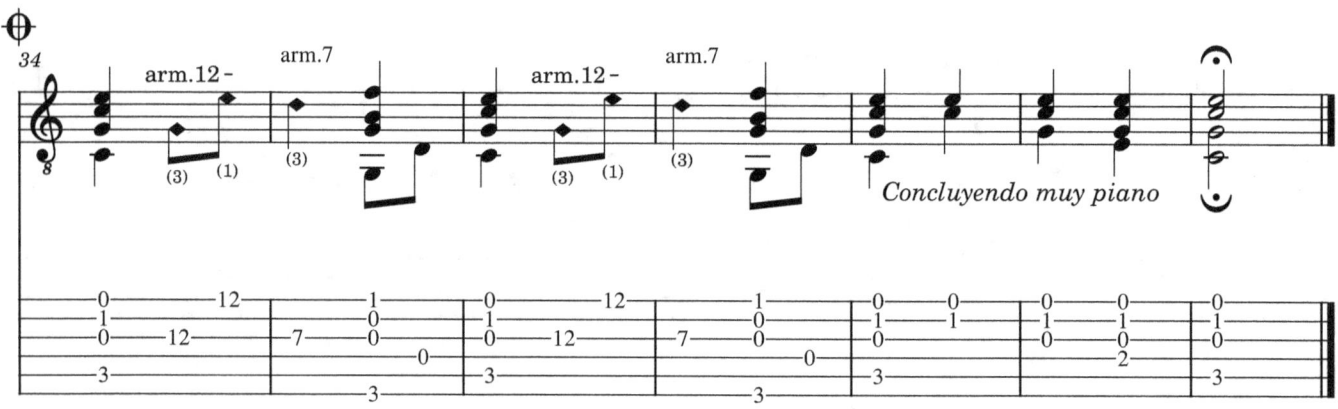

Polka

José Viñas (1823-1888)

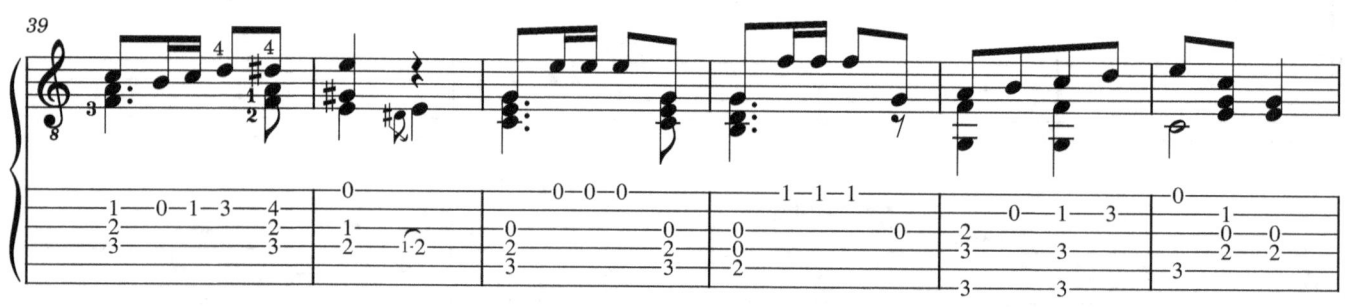

41

Francisco Tarrega (1852-1909)

Tárrega is considered to have laid the foundations for 20th century classical guitar and for increasing interest in the guitar as a recital instrument. Tárrega preferred small intimate performances over the concert stage. Some believe this was because he played without the nails needed for volume. Others say this was related to his childhood trauma.

Lagrima

Francisco Tarrega (1852-1909)

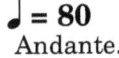
Andante.

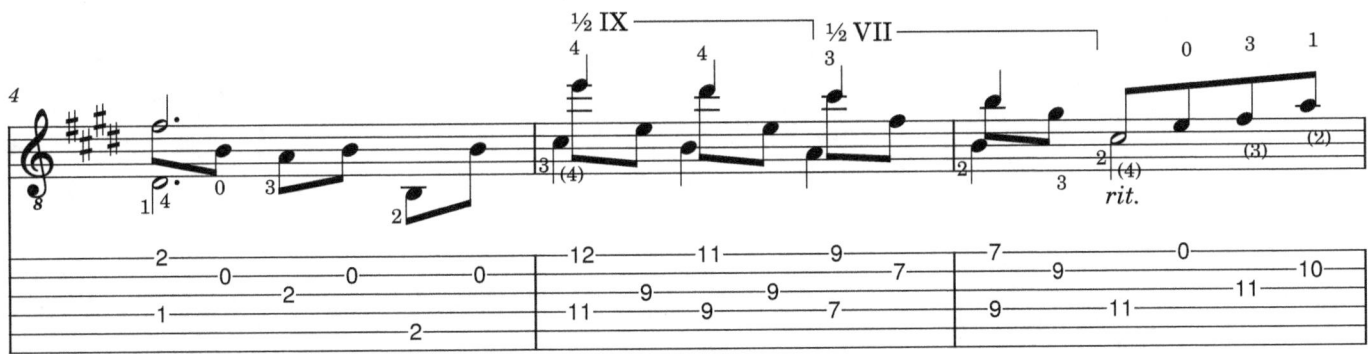

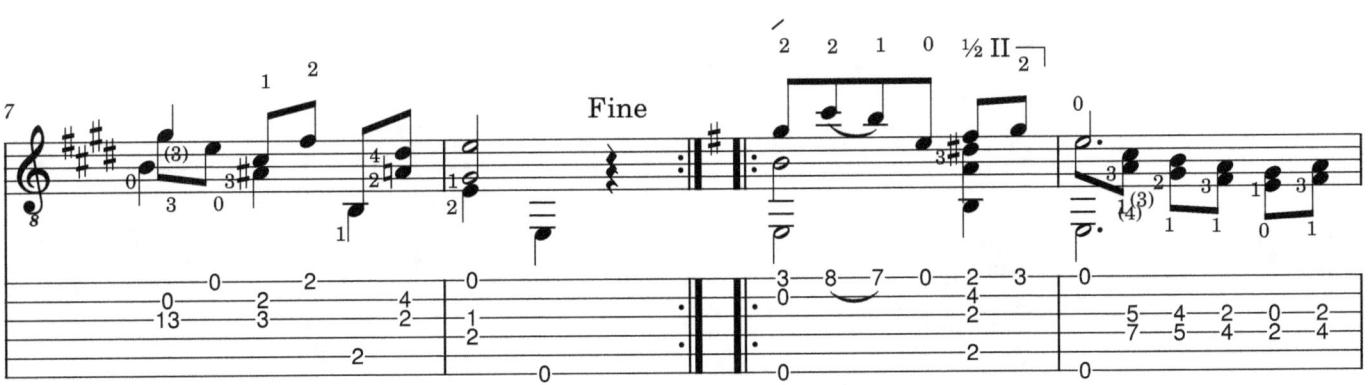

D.C. al Fine

Adelita

Mazurka

Francisco Tarrega (1852-1909)

Estudio

Francisco Tarrega

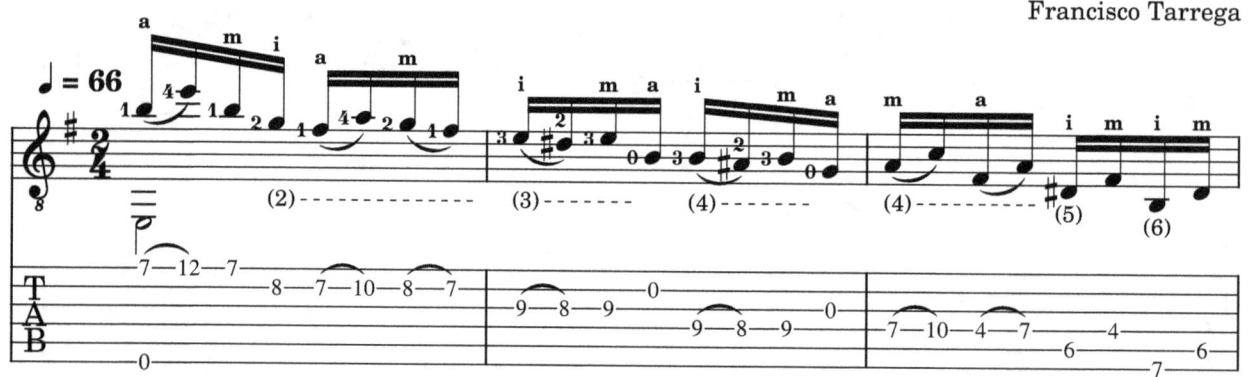
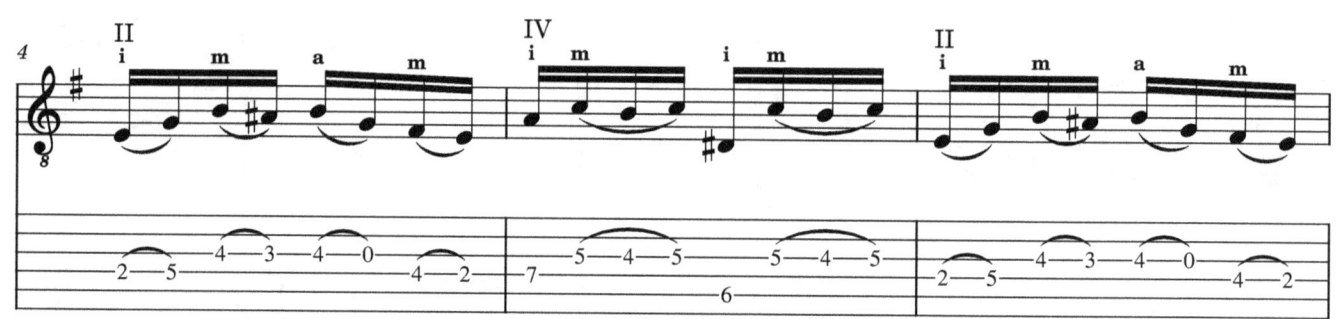
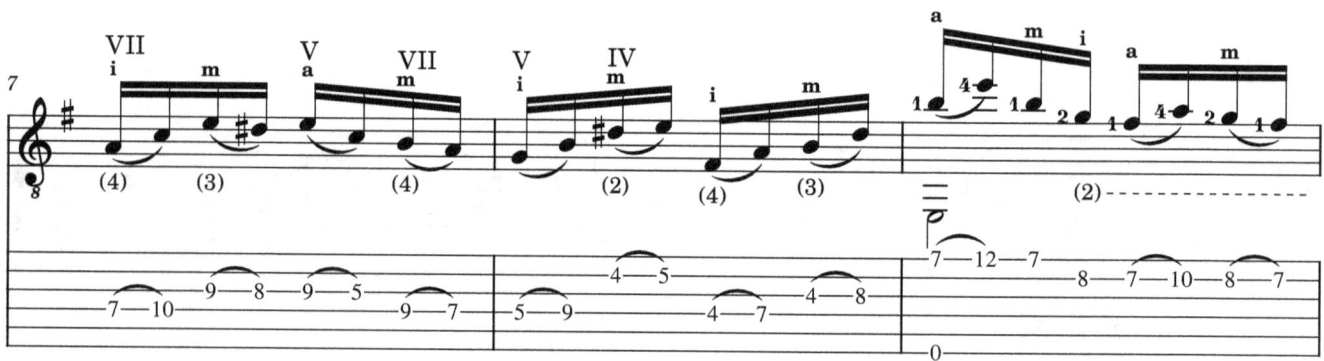
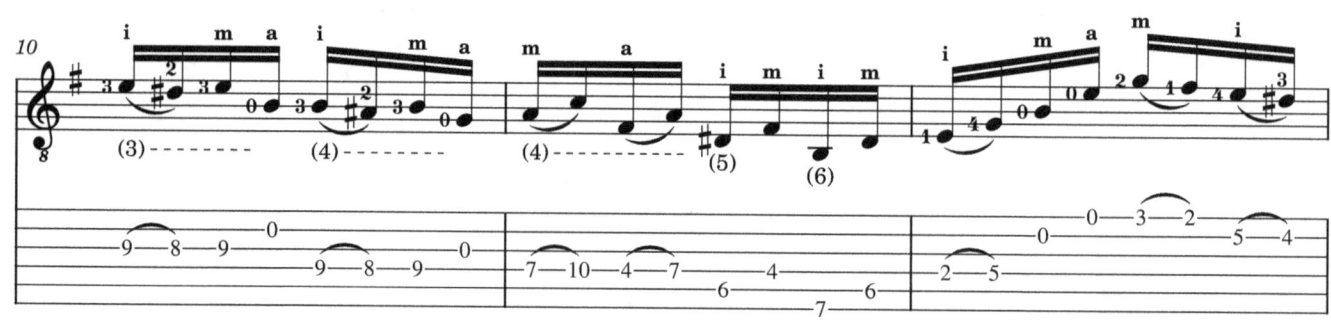

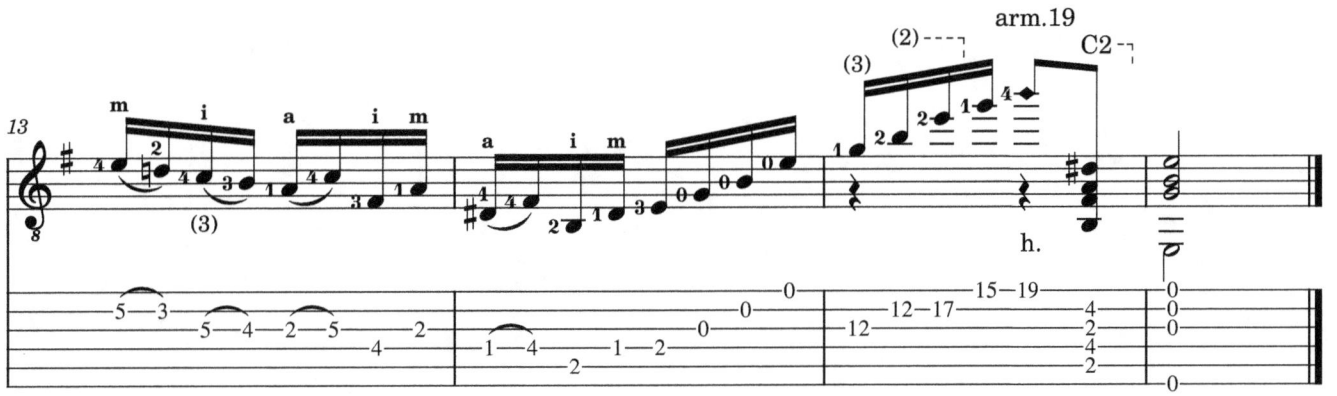

46

Etude

Francisco Tarrega (1852-1909)

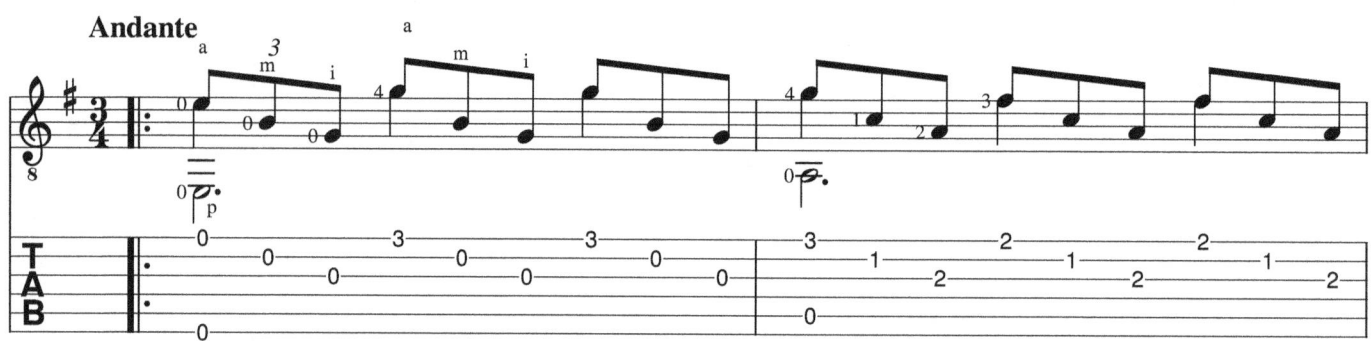

Etude No.1

Francisco Tarrega (1852-1909)

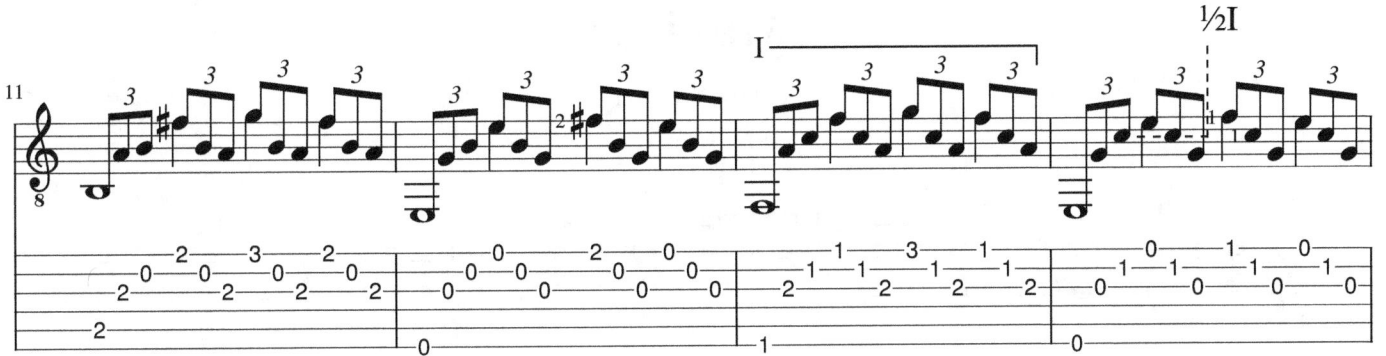

Marieta

Mazurka

Francisco Tárrega
(1852 - 1909)

Mazurka

En sol mayor

Francisco Tárrega
(1852 - 1909)

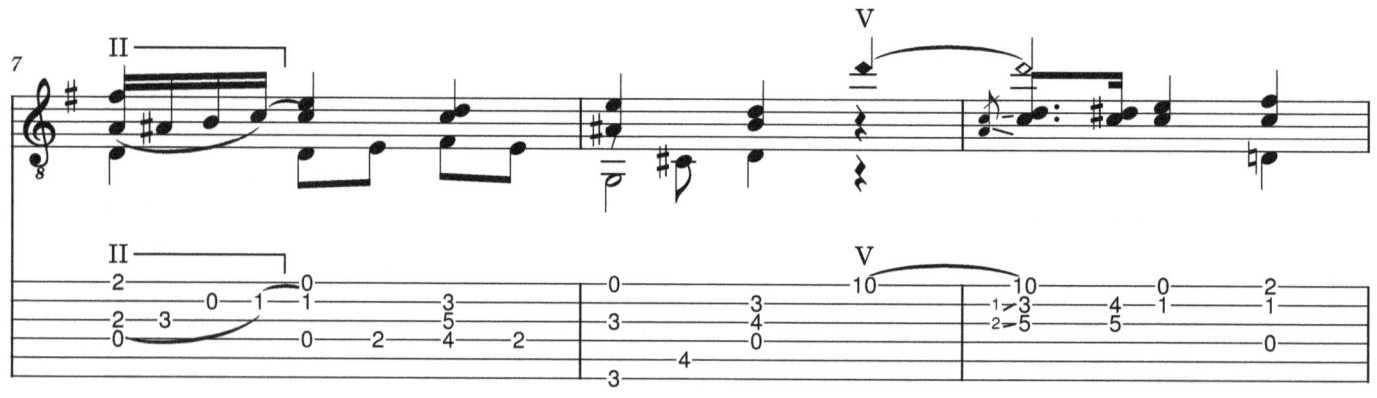
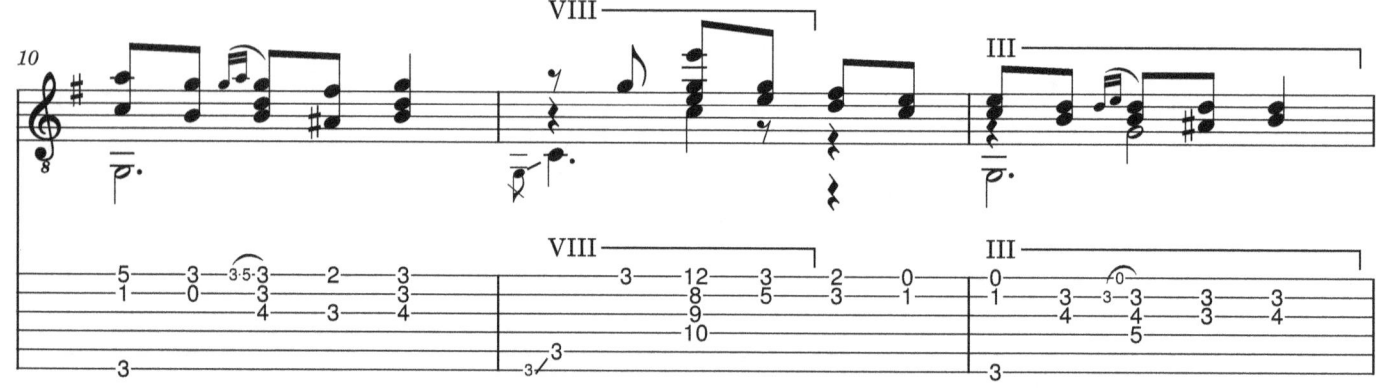

D.C. al Fine

Capricho Arabe
Serenata

Francisco Tárrega (1852 - 1909)

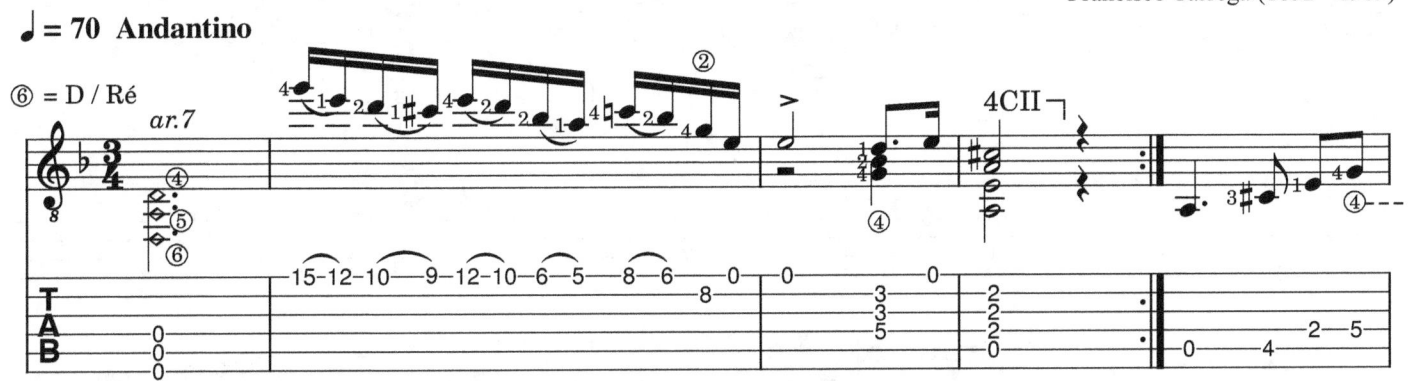

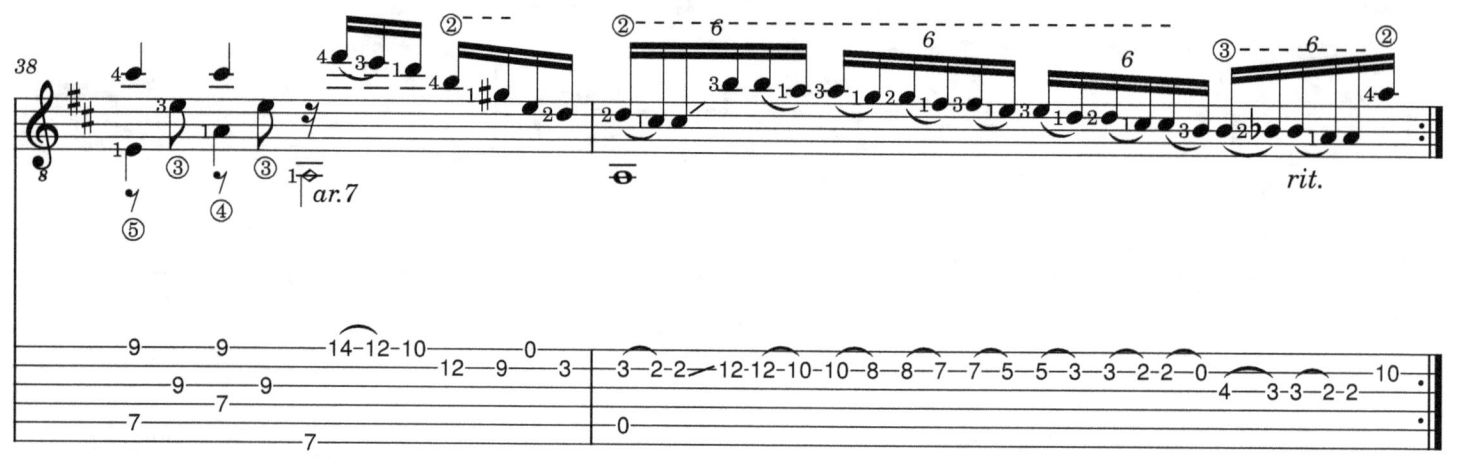
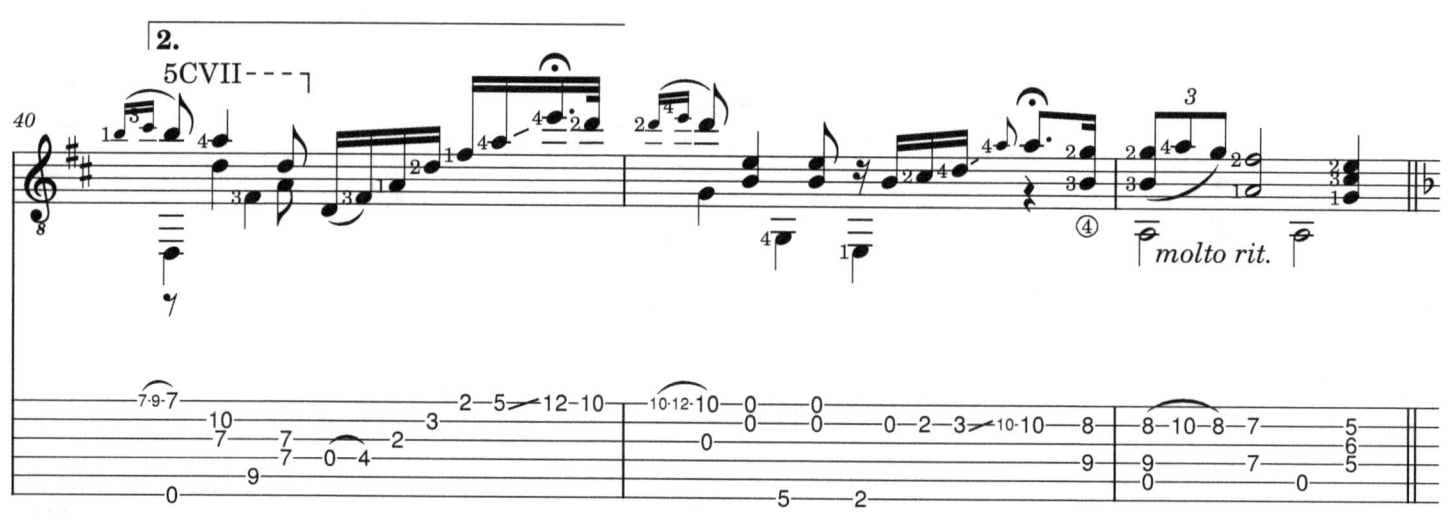
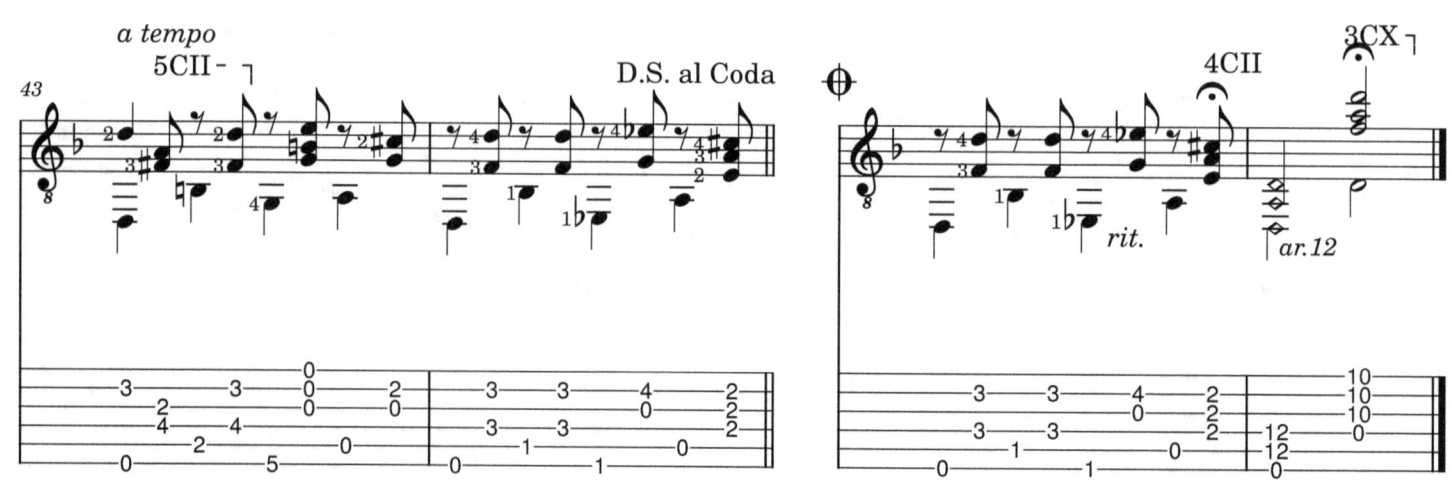

61

Miguel Llobet (1878 – 1938)

Miguel Llobet Solés was a classical guitarist, born in Barcelona, Spain.
Llobet was a renowned virtuoso who toured Europe and America extensively.
He made well known arrangements of Catalan folk songs for the solo guitar, made
famous arrangements for the guitar of the piano compositions of Isaac Albéniz,
arrangements immortalized by Andrés Segovia, and was also the composer of original works.

El Testament d'Amélia
Spanish Folk Song

Miguel Llobet (1878 –1938)

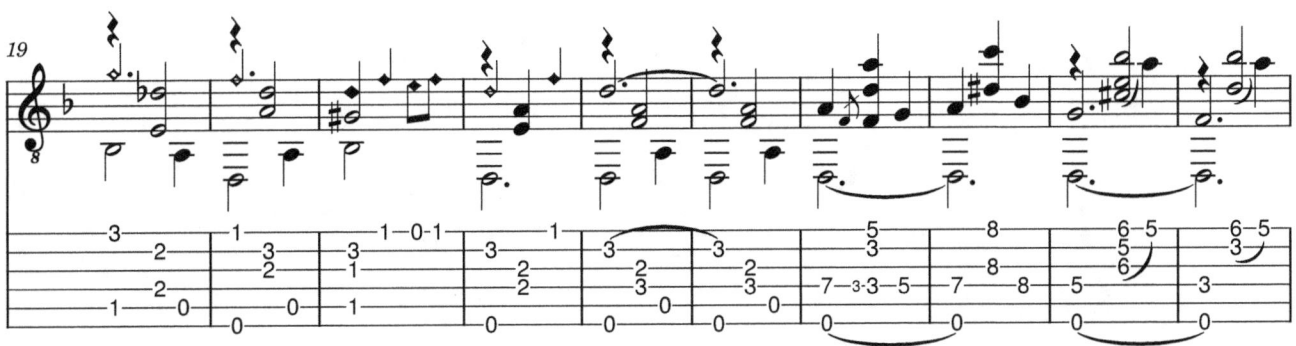

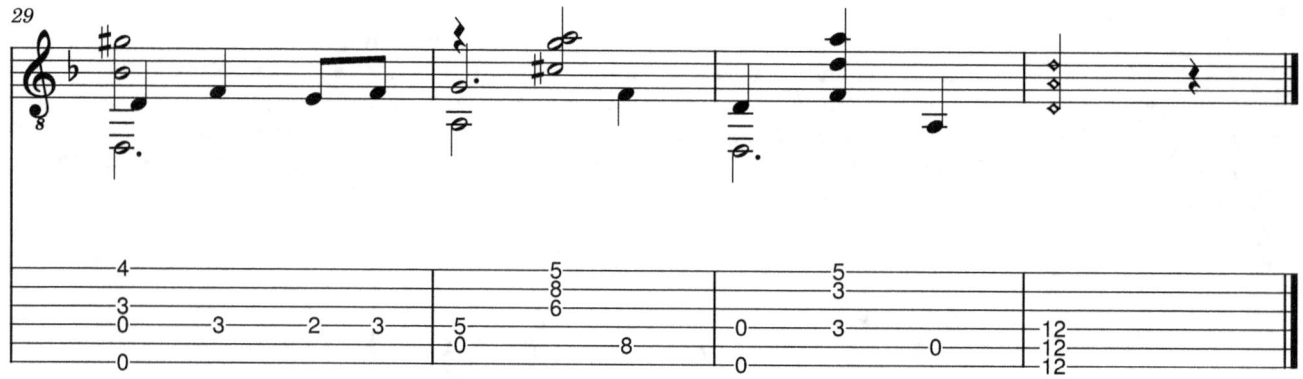

El Noi de la Mare
Cançó de Nadal catalana

Guitar arrangement by
Miguel Llobet (1878-1938)

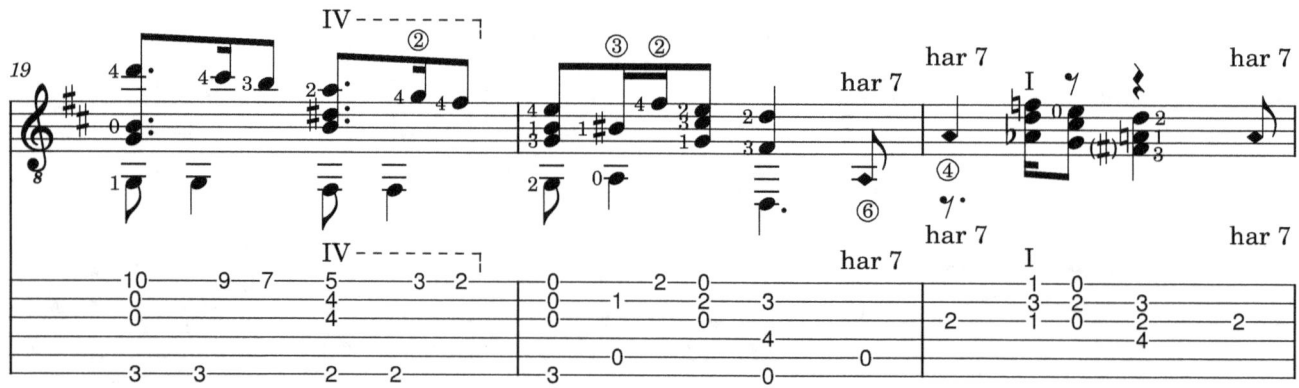
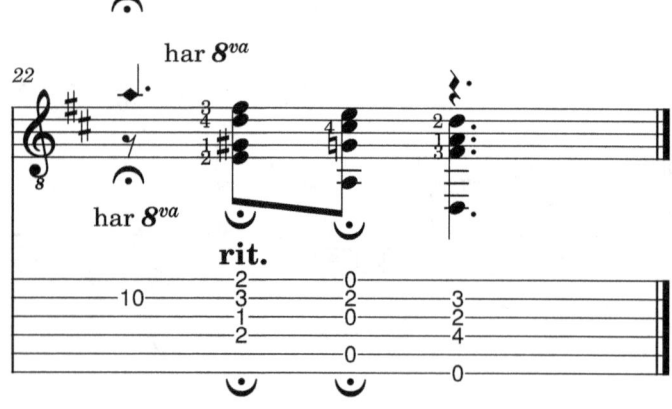

65

Leyenda

Isaac Albéniz (1860 –1909)

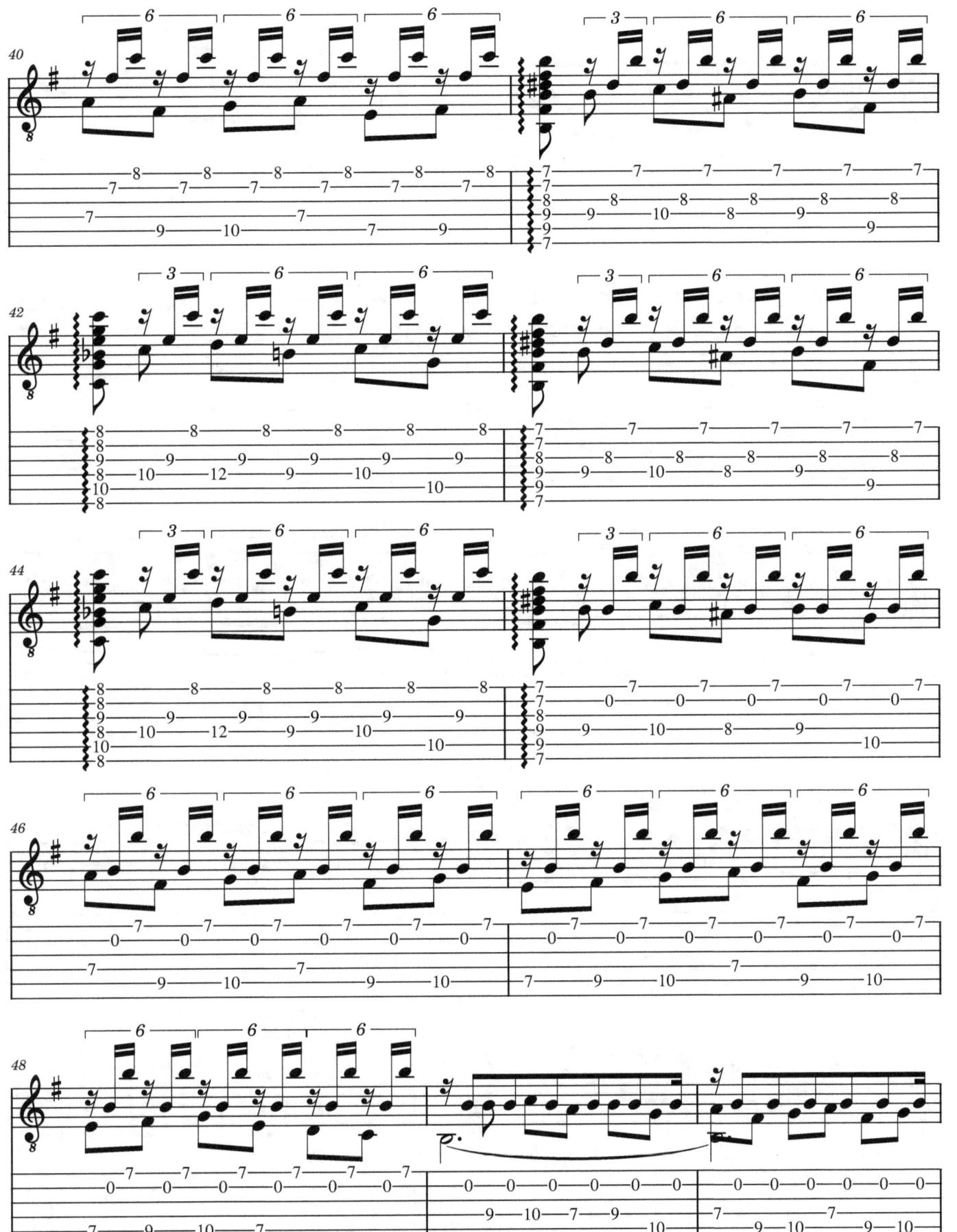

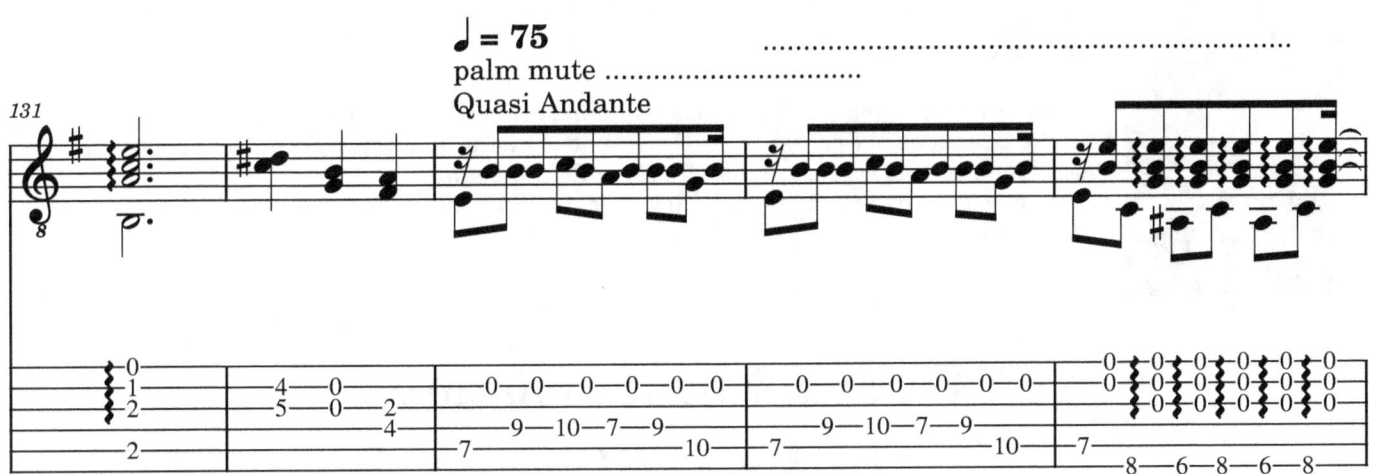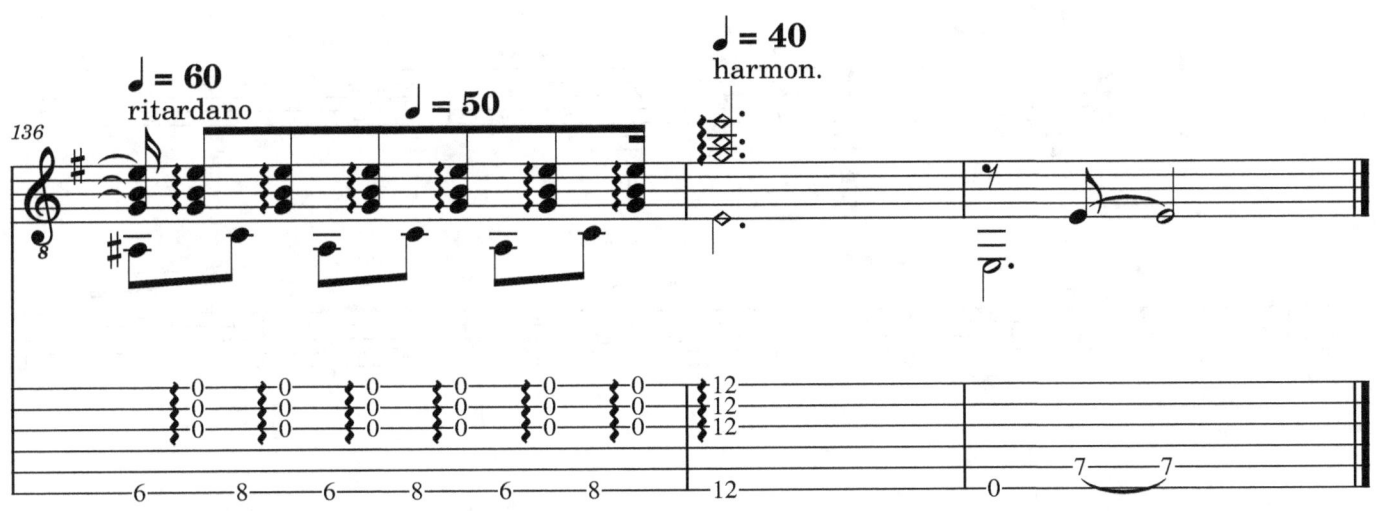

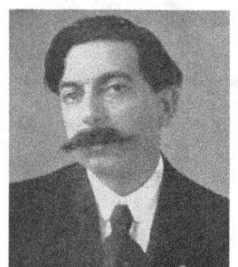

Enrique Granados (1867 -1916)

Pantaleón Enrique Joaquín Granados Campiña, commonly known as Enrique Granados in Spanish or Enric Granados in Catalan, was a Spanish composer of classical music, and concert pianist from Catalonia, Spain.
His most well-known works include Goyescas, the Spanish Dances, and María del Carmen.

3 Pieces without tablature

La Maja de Goya

(Tonadilla)

Enrique Granados (1867 – 1916)
(Trascription by Miguel Llobet)

Allegretto ♩. =60
6ª in Re
5ª in Sol

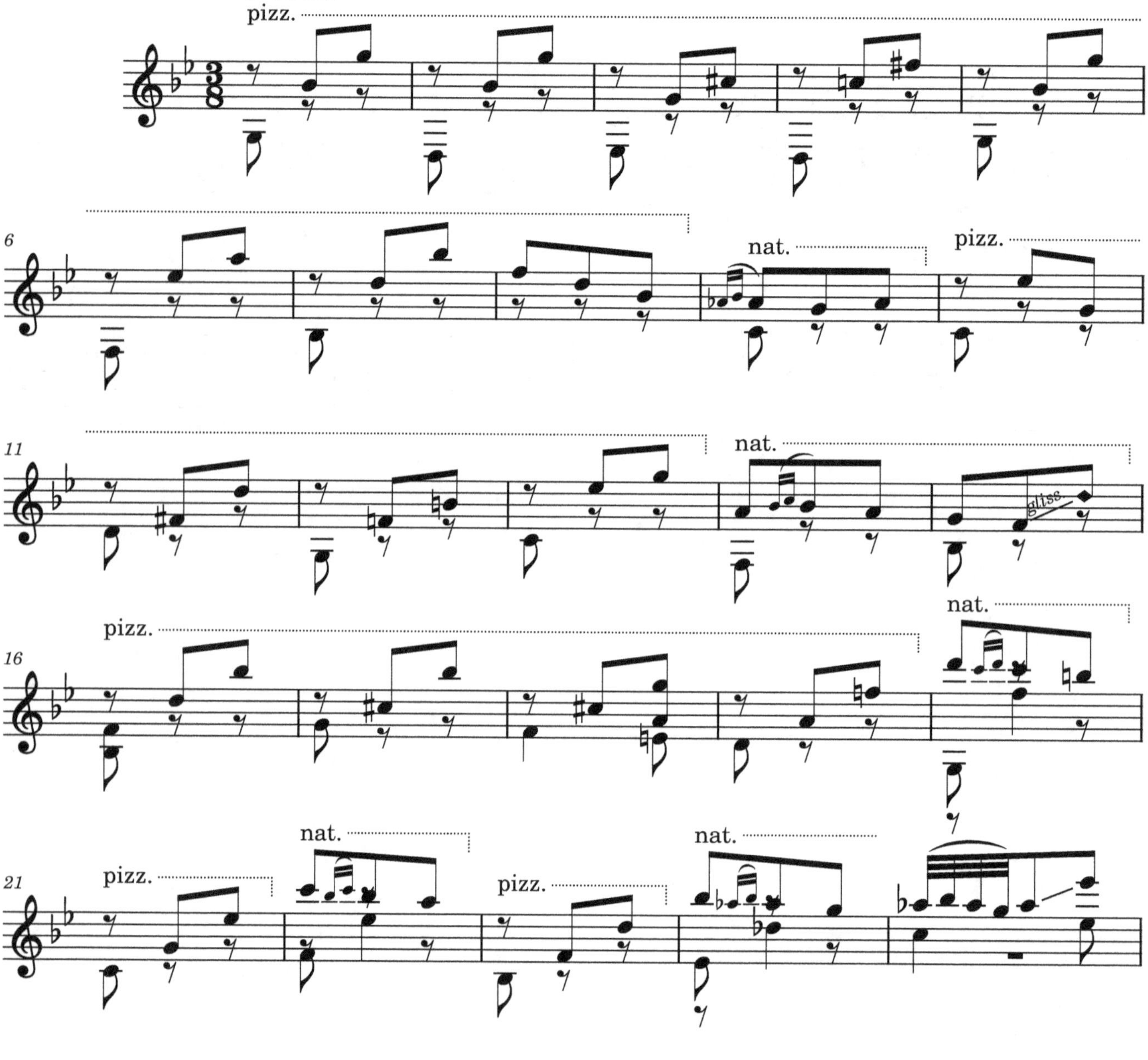

Andaluza
12 Danzas Españolas (Op. 37 No. 5)
Enrique Granados (1867-1916)

Serenata Española
No.2 from the 'Impresiones de España'

Joaquín Malats (1872-1912)

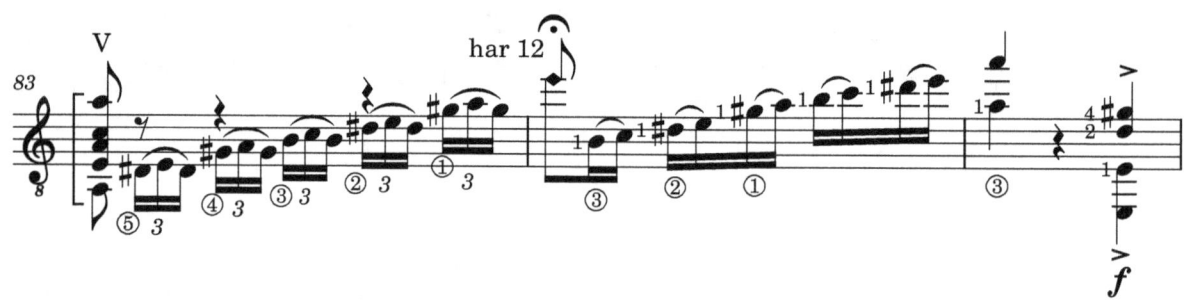

www.ingramcontent.com/pod-product-compliance
Lightning Source LLC
Chambersburg PA
CBHW081405070526
44583CB00020B/2689